THE Green Witchery
TAROT GUIDEBOOK

XX Judgment

Queen of Crystals

IX The Hermit

Cerridwen Greenleaf

CICO BOOKS

For my beloved Paul Velez.

Published in 2026 by CICO Books
An imprint of Ryland Peters & Small Ltd
20–21 Jockey's Fields   1452 Davis Bugg Road
London WC1R 4BW   Warrenton, NC 27589
www.rylandpeters.com
Email: euregulations@rylandpeters.com

10 9 8 7 6 5 4 3 2 1

Text © Brenda Knight 2026
Design and illustration © CICO Books 2026

The author's moral rights have been asserted. All rights reserved.
No part of this publication may be reproduced, stored in a retrieval system, or transmitted in any form or by any means, electronic, mechanical, photocopying, or otherwise, without the prior permission of the publisher.

A CIP record for this book is available
from the British Library.

US Library of Congress CIP data
has been applied for.

ISBN: 978-1-80065-591-1

Printed in China

Commissioning editor: Kristine Pidkameny
Senior designer: Emily Breen
Art director: Sally Powell
Creative director: Leslie Harrington
Production manager: Gordana Simakovic
Publishing manager: Carmel Edmonds

The authorised representative in the EEA is
Authorised Rep Compliance Ltd.,
Ground Floor, 71 Lower Baggot Street,
Dublin, D01 P593, Ireland
www.arccompliance.com

SAFETY NOTE

Please note that while the use of essential oils, herbs, incense, and particular practices may refer to healing benefits, they are not intended to replace diagnosis of illness or ailments, or healing or medicine. Always consult your doctor or other health professional in the case of illness. Essential oils are very powerful and potentially toxic if used too liberally. Follow the advice given on the label and never use the oils neat on bare skin, or if pregnant.

The safe and proper use of candles and incense is the sole responsibility of the person using them. Do not leave a burning candle unattended. Never burn a candle on or near anything that might catch fire. Keep candles out of the reach of children and pets.

Neither the author nor the publisher can be held responsible for any claim arising out of the general information and practices provided in this book.

MIX
Paper | Supporting
responsible forestry
FSC® C106563

Contents

Introduction 4
Using the Deck 5
The Spreads 6

   Daily Guidance: Single-Card Reading 6
   Swift Wisdom: Three-Card Reading 6
   Celtic Cross: Ten-Card Reading 8
   The Flower of Love: Eight-Card Reading 10
   Inner Garden: Five-Element Reading 12

The Major Arcana 13

   0 The Fool 14
   I The Magician 15
   II The High Priestess 16
   III The Empress 17
   IV The Emperor 18
   V The Hierophant 19
   VI The Lovers 20
   VII The Chariot 21
   VIII Strength 22
   IX The Hermit 23
   X The Wheel of Fortune 24
   XI Justice 25
   XII The Hanged Man 26
   XIII Death 27
   XIV Temperance 28
   XV The Devil 29
   XVI The Tower 30
   XVII The Star 31
   XVIII The Moon 32
   XIX The Sun 33
   XX Judgment 34
   XXI The World 35

Knight of Goblets

XIV Temperance

The Minor Arcana 36

   The Suit of Crystals 37
   The Suit of Athames 44
   The Suit of Wands 51
   The Suit of Goblets 58

Introduction

This deck weaves traditional Tarot with the wisdom of nature and invites you to forge a profound connection with Mother Earth through the practice of green witchery—a path of harmony, healing, and balance with nature, humanity, and your inner self. Each card is deeply researched and draws on the medieval origins of Tarot and hedgewitchery traditions, offering layered meanings through the language of flowers and pagan plant correspondences. The cards harness the energy of the natural world to guide you toward spiritual growth and personal insight.

The figures of the Major Arcana are accompanied by trees, herbs, and flowers, as well as tools of green witchery, and embody deep energies, astrological connections, and esoteric meanings. For example, The Hermit (see page 23), paired with night-blooming jasmine, signifies introspection and spiritual quests, while The Fool (see page 14), holding a white rose, symbolizes new beginnings and pure intentions.

The classic suits of the Minor Arcana are also presented through the lens of green witchery. While the suit of Wands keeps its namesake and is represented by budding branches, the suit of Cups becomes the suit of Goblets. Pentacles (or Coins) are transformed into Crystals, depicted as crystal balls, and Swords are shown as Athames—an athame is a green witch's knife used for magical purposes.

Whether you're new to Tarot or a seasoned reader, this deck offers a grounded way to tap into Earth's magic.

WHAT IS GREEN WITCHERY?

Green witchery or witchcraft is an earth-centered spiritual practice that reveres nature as a sacred source of magic and wisdom. Practitioners cultivate deep connections with plants, herbs, crystals, animals, and seasonal cycles, using herbalism, foraging, and rituals to harness natural energies for spells, potions, and healing. Rooted in ancient traditions like Celtic and Indigenous wisdom, it emphasizes living sustainably and intuitively, without rigid dogma. The benefits include profound personal healing—physical, emotional, and spiritual—through natural remedies; heightened intuition and inner balance; a sense of empowerment via self-reliance; and fostering environmental stewardship, promoting harmony with the planet for our collective well-being. Green witchery is the most practical magic of all.

Using the Deck

These cards will help you foster balance, heal, and grow, embracing the green witch's path of stewardship and reverence for Mother Nature's abundant gifts.

1 **Set Your Intention and Energy:** Choose a spread (see pages 6–12) and ground yourself before you start. Hold the deck, take deep breaths, and focus on your question or intention. Green witchery is informed by the five elements—Earth, Water, Fire, Air, and Spirit—which form a sacred foundation to connect with the natural world. It thrives on Earth's energy, so consider reading outdoors or near plants to amplify the connection. You may also choose to light incense (see Swift Wisdom on page 6).

2 **Shuffle and Draw:** Shuffle the deck while keeping your question in mind. Pulling the cards from the top of the newly shuffled deck, draw the number of cards required for your chosen spread and lay them out face down in front of you. When you are doing a reading for another person (the querent), have them shuffle the cards gently and thoroughly until you sense that their energy is in the card deck.

3 **Interpret the Cards:** Turn over the cards one by one. Explore the card meanings on pages 13–64, paying attention to plant symbolism. For example, The World, with its bountiful garden imagery, signals the completion of a life cycle, encouraging gratitude and rest.

4 **Reflect and Apply:** Journal your readings to track insights. This deck encourages self-reflection and action, helping you to align your life with nature's rhythms.

5 **Storing the Deck:** When not in use, keep the cards in something made from a natural material, like a cotton pouch or wooden box, to honor their earthy essence.

The Spreads

Choose a spread that fits your needs or those of your querent, the person for whom you are doing the reading.

Daily Guidance: Single-Card Reading

The simplest reading you can perform is to work with a single card to answer the question, "What do I need to know today?" Shuffle and draw your card as described on page 5.

As well as interpreting the card's meaning on pages 13–64, you can explore the practice offered. For example, if you draw The Hermit, you could anoint your wrists with jasmine oil and take a mindfulness walk. These simple rituals allow you to deepen your connection with the cards' messages.

Swift Wisdom: Three-Card Reading

We all have moments when we need really good advice and wise counsel as soon as we can get it. This spread is perfect for that. You will gain clarity to help you make decisions and work out your next steps. The cards offer insight into the past, present, and future.

Choose a peaceful space for the reading where you can be in solitude and avoid any interruptions—full concentration is required, especially since time is of the essence. As well as the deck, you will need a pen and paper, matches, a white candle, a fireproof dish, and a calming incense stick, such as jasmine or lavender. Place the deck in front of the candle and incense. Light the incense and walk around the room with it to cleanse the space, then place the stick in the fireproof dish. Light the candle and sit down. Breathe in deeply and exhale fully three times. Now you can begin.

Gently and thoroughly shuffle the deck to make sure there is no lingering energy from previous readings. Once well shuffled, pass the deck over the incense widdershins (counterclockwise) with your right hand. This ritual serves as an invocation for wisdom direct from Source (Mother Earth, the source of all green witchery wisdom).

Using your left hand, pick two batches of cards from the deck to make three stacks. Do this quickly to allow your unconscious mind to guide the dividing of the deck and the creation of the three stacks. Pick up the top card from each stack and place them face down in a row on the table in front of the candle and incense. Turn over the first card to discover your first message from Source. This card relates to the past. Write down the card and your immediate

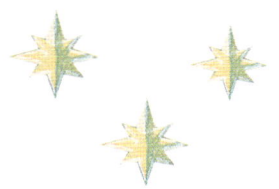 

understanding from the card. Do the same with the next two cards, which relate to the present and future.

Record the date and time of the reading and consider the swift wisdom you have received. Take the candle and incense into your bedroom and extinguish them before you go to sleep.

Place your notes on your nightstand and look at them again when you awaken in the morning. You will know what to do now. Give thanks to the wisdom of Source, which we return to again and again for grace and guidance in our lives.

1 Past   2 Present   3 Future

The Spreads **7**

Celtic Cross: Ten-Card Reading

Rooted in nineteenth-century mysticism, the Celtic Cross spread weaves a narrative of your journey, blending past, present, and future with inner and outer influences, offering timeless wisdom. It can be used for any question for which you or the querent need in-depth guidance.

Hold the deck while envisioning roots grounding you to the Earth. Focus on the question, shuffling hand-over-hand or riffling gently until your intuition signals you to stop. Cut the deck into three stacks, reassemble, then draw ten cards. Lay them out as shown, and then turn over and interpret each card as indicated opposite.

When you have finished reading the cards, anoint your wrists with a drop of lavender essential oil and meditate on your goals.

EXAMPLE READING

What guidance does the Universe offer me for personal growth?

1. **Present:** The Fool—You are embracing a new beginning with optimism.
2. **Challenge:** Four of Goblets—You feel stuck, needing to reflect on past joys.
3. **Past:** The Hermit—Introspection has shaped your wisdom.
4. **Future:** Ten of Goblets—Joyful connections await you.
5. **Conscious goal:** The World—You are seeking closure and rewards.
6. **Subconscious:** Ace of Crystals—Abundance is driving you.
7. **Attitude:** Three of Wands—You are planning boldly with optimism.
8. **Environment:** Seven of Athames—Deceptive influences are surrounding you.
9. **Hopes/fears:** The Star—You hope for healing, but fear vulnerability.
10. **Outcome:** Eight of Crystals—Dedication will yield growth for you.

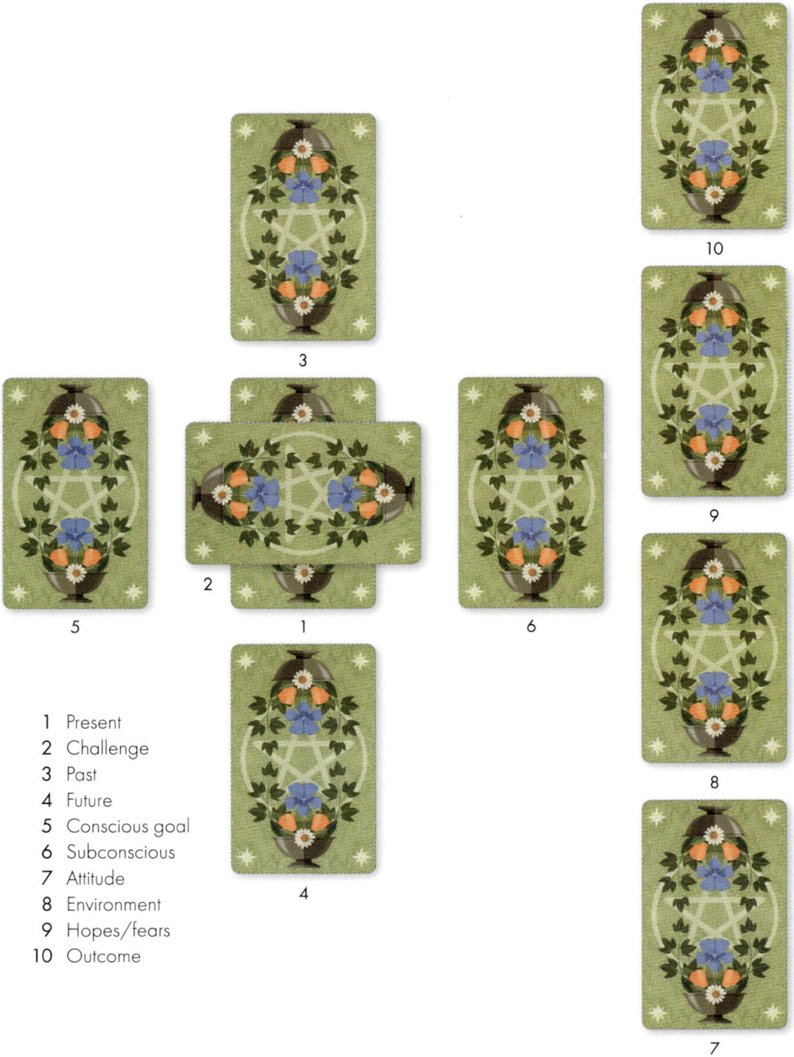

1. Present
2. Challenge
3. Past
4. Future
5. Conscious goal
6. Subconscious
7. Attitude
8. Environment
9. Hopes/fears
10. Outcome

The Flower of Love: Eight-Card Reading

The Flower of Love is an eight-card tarot layout, forming a flower shape to explore every facet of love, from a new romantic attraction to long-term relationships. Cards 1 (center) and 2–7 (petals) create a circular bloom, with Card 8 (stem) at the bottom, grounding the reading.

Lay out the cards as shown opposite, then turn over and interpret each card as indicated.

When you have finished reading the cards, gather a rose or another flower and place in view to take in the scent while ruminating on what the cards have revealed.

EXAMPLE READING

What do I need to know about my new love?

The flower center:

1 The Star—Hope and renewal drive new love. Trust divine timing for a fresh romantic start.

The petals:

2 Five of Goblets—Past heartbreak clouds emotions. Release sorrow to see new love's potential.

3 Nine of Crystals—Heal through self-love. Independence attracts healthy new love.

4 Ace of Wands—A spark of attraction ignites. Embrace bold, passionate new love.

5 The Hermit—Introspection clarifies romantic desires. Seek inner truth for true love.

6 Knight of Wands—Passion drives bold action. Pursue new love with enthusiasm, but stay balanced.

7 Seven of Athames—Protect your heart with boundaries. Be wary of dishonesty in new love.

The stem:

8 Ten of Crystals—Build lasting love through trust and shared values. Take practical steps.

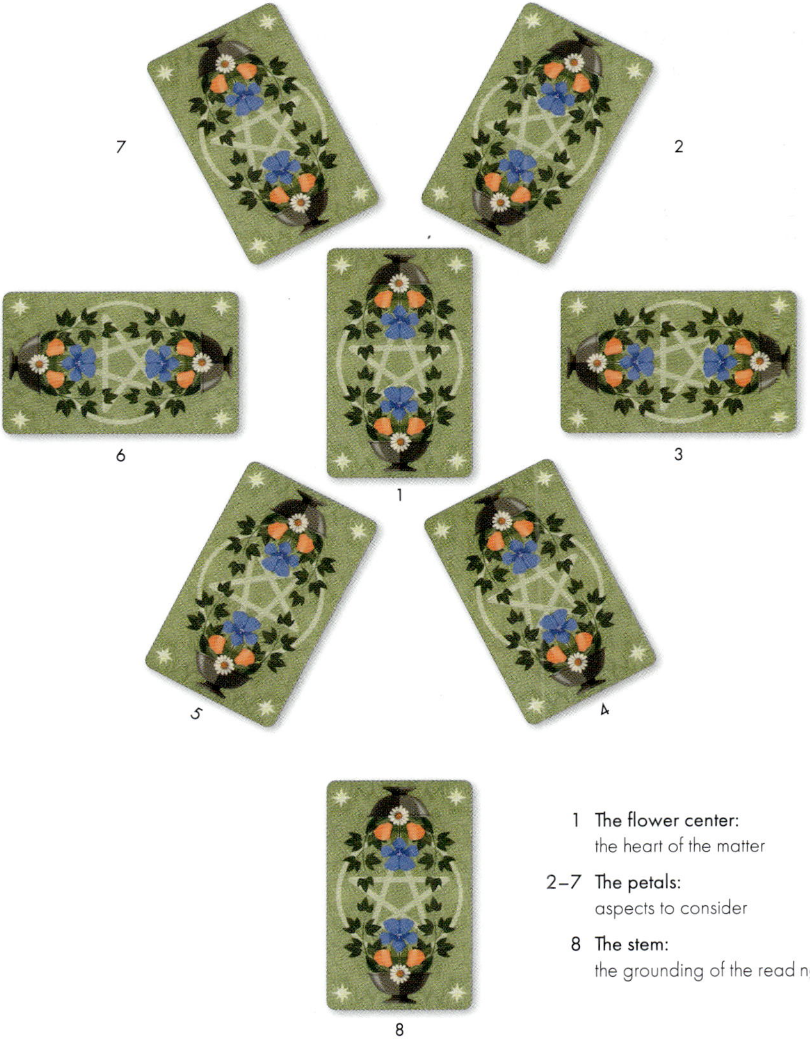

1. **The flower center:**
   the heart of the matter

2–7 **The petals:**
   aspects to consider

8. **The stem:**
   the grounding of the reading

The Spreads **11**

Inner Garden: Five-Element Reading

3 Fire: passion

4 Air: mind

5 Spirit: core

2 Water: emotions

1 Earth: foundation

This spread allows you to align with elemental harmony—Earth, Water, Fire, Air, and Spirit. Each card guides the querent to cultivate inner peace through nature's balance, rooted in Earth's cycles.

Hold the deck, visualizing a blooming garden within. Shuffle hand-over-hand or riffle gently, focusing on the question. Stop when intuition guides you, cut into three stacks, reassemble, and draw five cards. Lay them out as shown, then turn over and interpret each card as indicated.

When you have finished reading the cards, plant marigolds, share jasmine tea with loved ones, and meditate under stars to embody hope.

EXAMPLE READING

How can I nurture inner peace?

1. **Earth (foundation):** Ace of Crystals—You are grounding peace in practical self-care, building a stable base.

2. **Water (emotions):** Ten of Goblets—Emotional fulfillment through love and community nurtures your heart.

3. **Fire (passion):** Three of Wands—Your drive for growth fuels inner calm through inspired action.

4. **Air (mind):** Four of Goblets—Reflecting on past joys can clear your mind for peace.

5. **Spirit (core):** The Star—Hope and healing are guiding you to spiritual serenity.

The Major Arcana

There are 22 cards in the Major Arcana, which are said to relate the journey of card 0, The Fool (see page 14), through life, culminating in celebration in card XXI, The World (see page 35). In this deck you will find added layers of meaning indicated by the tools of green witchery, such as herbs and flowers. The Major Arcana cards are connected to the element of Spirit.

Each card includes a description and an explanation of its meaning. If you are drawing these cards for a single-card pull (see page 6), there is also guidance—a concise call to action—and a practice, which suggests a way of incorporating that card's energy into your day.

0 The Fool

V The Hierophant

XII The Hanged Man

XXI The World

0 The Fool

White Budding Rose of Possibility

0 The Fool

The Fool, carrying all his belongings in a small pouch and standing on a precipice, may look foolish to the world, but could possibly be the wisest of all. His white rose evinces unlimited potential and a childlike trust in what is to come. His garb is also bestrewn with colorful roses. The small dog by his side signifies the spirit of freedom, new beginnings, and adventure. This beloved Major Arcana card conveys youthful optimism, an open mind, and an adventurous willingness to take the leap into an unknown future.

Meaning: This card can connote all of the qualities of The Fool's character as well as purity, freedom, and new beginnings. Most significantly of all, this card can indicate purity of intention. Believe in your innate wisdom. If you are feeling hesitant or indecisive about something in your life, the appearance of The Fool in your reading is reminding you that you have the chance for a fresh start.

Practice: Choose a white flower from your garden or from a local florist. Place the flower somewhere you will see it frequently during the day. As you gaze at it, consider all the good things that lie ahead for you in your life.

GUIDANCE

Take a leap of faith. Decide YES.

I The Magician
Manifestation and Mastery

A striking figure stands at a wooden altar surrounded by vibrant nasturtium and basil, which symbolize creativity and abundance. The Magician holds a wand of protective rowan wood skyward, channeling energy. Four elemental tools—a feather (Air), a candle (Fire), a stone (Earth), and a shell (Water)—rest on the altar, representing mastery over life's forces, alongside a chalice filled with the life-giving renewal of rainwater. In the background, a grove of magical hawthorn trees blooms under a radiant midday sun, evoking inspiration and transformation.

Meaning: The Magician embodies the power of creation, resourcefulness, and focused intention. It signifies your ability to harness your skills, intuition, and the elements around you to manifest your desires. Channel your talents and focus your energy, like the figure wielding the wand. Trust in your ability to transform ideas into action. Listen to your inner spark, align your mind, heart, and resources, and take bold steps toward your goals.

Practice: Gather a nasturtium flower (or an orange item) and a small stone. Sit at a clear space, place the items before you, and light a candle to symbolize fire. Visualize a white light flowing through you, connecting your intention to the elements. Breathe deeply, affirming, "I manifest my vision with clarity and power." Carry the stone as a talisman to anchor your creative energy.

I The Magician

GUIDANCE

The Universe is ready to support your vision—act with confidence.

II The High Priestess
Serene Silence and Great Wisdom

GUIDANCE

You are being called to attain your higher self. The time has come for you to evolve.

The appearance of The High Priestess brings good omens when she appears in readings, as well as a reminder to trust your intuition and the guidance of the divine feminine. Her long, flowing robe is adorned with embroidered purple iris, the flower of wisdom. She holds a wand tipped with a violet, a symbol of insight. The pillars of her temple are decorated with purple blossoms, too. The High Priestess has studied and mastered many subjects and has delved into many secrets. She is wisdom personified.

Meaning: This card can represent an aspect of you growing in self-understanding. The High Priestess can also be a harbinger of an important new woman arriving in your life. Gaining knowledge from learned women can be a key to your spiritual expansion. However, exploring the obscure and arcane takes time and immense solitude. Retreat and spend time with yourself; you need to turn inward to do the work required for self-development.

Practice: In a quiet place, sit in a comfortable position with your back held straight and close your eyes. Start by inhaling and exhaling a few times. Visualize a beautiful blue circle. As you meditate, observe how the blue circle is expanding. Soon, it will be an intensely exquisite violet-blue. Spend 11 minutes (11 is a master number, which is about spiritual understanding and seeking higher purposes) in this reverie every day and you will indeed deepen your understanding of yourself and your potential. Blessed be!

III The Empress
Earth Goddess Energy

The Empress is an earth goddess bathed in golden light in a lush garden of tuberose, calla lilies, red roses, hydrangeas, and sunflowers. She graces your reading with radiant warmth, a symbol of abundance and nurturing. A wise caretaker, The Empress embodies the beauty of creation, tending to life with compassion and grace. She is the heartbeat of love and fertility.

Meaning: The Empress signifies a time of creation, where your ideas, relationships, or dreams flourish. She may reflect your own blossoming creativity or herald the arrival of a loving, supportive figure. Her presence in a reading is a reminder of the capacity to nurture and grow: this is a moment to trust in abundance and to honor your inner wellspring of love. The Empress asks you to sow seeds of kindness with tenderness and watch them bloom. Seek inspiration in nature or loving souls, and trust in your ability to bring beauty to life.

Practice: Stand barefoot, so you feel the grass and earth under your feet and breathe deeply, grounding yourself. Close your eyes and envision a lush garden bathed in golden light, with vibrant flowers blooming around you. Feel the earth goddess energy nourishing your heart.

III The Empress

GUIDANCE

Embrace your nurturing side to cultivate beauty, growth, harmony, and connection.

IV The Emperor

Pillar of Authority

IV The Emperor

GUIDANCE

Take charge of your path. You have the power to shape your world.

A regal figure sits upon a stone throne, adorned with ram's heads, his crimson robe flowing like a river of resolve. In his left hand, he holds a golden orb, symbol of dominion; in the right, an ankh, the key of life. Behind this imposing figure is a wall of green bamboo, grown closely together as a symbol of power, protection, and wealth. The Emperor represents the gift of stability through leadership. A beacon of structure, he embodies discipline and protection, ruling with unwavering clarity.

Meaning: The Emperor enters your reading with a commanding presence, reflecting your own strength or the influence of a steadfast, guiding figure. He signifies a time of order and control, where structure paves the way for progress. The Emperor invites you to harness your inner authority, build foundations with intention and strength, and stand firm in your truth. Seek wisdom from those who embody discipline and integrity, and lead with confidence, whether through clear goals, firm boundaries, or decisive action.

Practice: Take a sage smudge stick and fireproof dish and find a quiet space where you can sit tall, grounding yourself. Light the smudge stick and breathe deeply, feeling strength rise within you. Close your eyes and think about your goals for deepening your inner work on your path to a peaceful and joyful life.

V The Hierophant
Wisdom Through Sacred Connection

Seated on a throne is The Hierophant, draped in robes embroidered with sage and lavender, herbs of purification and insight. At this solemn figure's feet, nasturtium and alyssum bloom, radiating peace and healing. Two sturdy pillars, entwined with ivy and dotted with violet blossoms, frame the scene, representing structure and divine wisdom.

Meaning: The Hierophant embodies spiritual guidance, tradition, and the pursuit of deeper truths. Like The Chariot (see page 21), it emphasizes inner harmony, but here the focus is on connecting with sacred wisdom and communal values. You are called to embrace teachings that resonate with your soul, whether from tradition, mentors, or inner reflection. The Hierophant asks you to balance respect for knowledge from trusted sources with personal discernment. Trust in the stability of your values to guide you and seek community or ritual to deepen your understanding.

Practice: When you are seeking inner wisdom, meditate with lavender. Find a chair in your home that represents power for you and sit in stillness for 5–10 minutes, as you hold a sprig of lavender and breathe deeply. Visualize a violet light filling your mind with clarity, then reflect on a particular question or truth you seek. Journal your insights and keep a sprig of lavender as a reminder of your spiritual connection.

V The Hierophant

GUIDANCE

This is a time to learn, grow, anc align with your higher purpose.

VI The Lovers
Reclaiming Eden

GUIDANCE

The choices you make in the early stages of a commitment determine its future.

Portrayed in an Edenic scene, a man and a woman hold hands under a splendidly sunny sky, just as Adam and Eve would have been before the Fall. An angelic being with large, radiant wings casts a watchful eye over them. The Lovers are surrounded by abundant fruit trees bearing apples and oranges, reminders of the garden of Eden.

Meaning: You will soon need to make a significant decision about a central relationship in your life. As this card hints broadly, this choice is frequently a matter of the heart. Just like in Eden, choices made determine the future. As an example, if you are overly self-sacrificing, that will set a pattern where that behavior is expected going forward. The same applies for non-romantic commitments: This is the time when you need to decide if you are all in—if you are dedicated. The Lovers can also simply indicate union. If you are in a budding relationship, romantic or otherwise, it is very likely to be a major one in your life and a true partnership of harmony and balance.

Practice: Self-love can help prevent over-giving, which can lead to imbalance in all relationships, not just romantic love. To boost self-esteem, create your own affirmations. Make a magical ink by mashing up a palmful of raspberries, which contain love magic, in a bowl with a splash of apple cider vinegar. Use the magical ink to write an affirmation on a strip of paper and keep it on a table or your altar. Write a new affirmation every day for a more joy-filled, ebullient life.

VII The Chariot
Growth Through Inner Harmony

A confident female figure stands tall in a sturdy chariot crafted from oak, symbolizing strength and endurance, and decorated with ivy for rebirth, willow branches for flexibility, and a pink clover flower, indicating balance and harmony. Her tunic is adorned with a vibrant sprig of rosemary and her hair with bay laurel. Two majestic wolves, one white and one black, are drawing the chariot and represent the balance of opposing forces. In the background, a river lined with water lilies flows calmly, reflecting the charioteer's focused yet serene state of mind.

Meaning: This exhilarating card embodies disciplined willpower and self-mastery, as well as the drive to move forward with purpose. Like The High Priestess (see page 16), it calls for inner alignment, but here it's about channeling that wisdom into action. Take the reins of your life with confidence. The botanical elements emphasize grounding and clarity amid challenges, urging you to harness both intuition and determination to guide your path. Balance your emotions and logic, like the two wolves pulling in harmony.

Practice: Sunflowers are in constant motion during the day. Slowly and surely, they follow the Sun from dawn to dusk (a process known as heliotropism). Upon sunrise, take a budding sunflower in a vase, set it in a window, and greet the day with a prayer for foreword movement in your life. At nightfall, place the sunflower on a table or your altar and speak your gratitude out loud.

VII The Chariot

GUIDANCE

The time for hesitation is over—move forward with focus. You are able to overcome all obstacles.

VIII Strength
Courage Through Compassion

A majestic lion is cradled by a gentle woman wearing a crown of sunflowers, symbolizing vitality and inner power. Her flowing cloak is woven with threads of nettle and rose, representing resilience and love. A sturdy oak tree looms in the background, its roots entwined with wild thyme, grounding the scene in strength and endurance. Above, a golden sun shines brightly, casting a warm glow that reflects the woman's calm yet unwavering resolve.

Meaning: The quiet power of inner courage, compassion, and self-control is embodied by this radiant card. It speaks to taming fears and challenges, not through force, but through understanding. Like the figure soothing the lion, approach difficulties with patience rather than aggression. The botanical and animal imagery underscores the harmony of fierceness and gentleness, urging you to trust your inner resilience to overcome obstacles with grace.

Practice: Nurture inner strength by placing a sunflower petal (or a small sunflower) and a sprig of thyme on your altar before you. Light a candle to represent the Sun's energy. Hold the thyme, visualizing its grounding strength filling you. Then, touch the sunflower, imagining its warmth fueling your courage. Sit comfortably with your eyes closed for 11 minutes and focus on a challenge you are facing, envisioning yourself meeting it with calm resolve. (The number 11 is a master number—see the Practice on page 16.) Keep the thyme as a talisman for resilience.

GUIDANCE
Embrace vulnerability as a source of power, and let love—for yourself and others—be your anchor.

IX The Hermit
Lighting the Way Forward

A robed old man stands illuminated by a starry night sky, holding a staff and a lantern as he searches for wisdom and enlightenment. The inner work of pursuing self-understanding can only be done alone; the deep work of self-reflection and introspective soul work is a solo quest. The Hermit walks a spiritual path which is lined with night-blooming jasmine. The beautiful flowers produce a scent that is redolent of an intense aliveness, a lovely perfume that signals peacefulness and reminds this green witch of the loving generosity of Mother Earth. The wisdom arising from this journey is a light in the darkness.

Meaning: Now is the time to seek wisdom. Regard The Hermit as a sign you need to take a retreat or withdraw to spend time in contemplation. The appearance of this wanderer in your reading is also an indication of timing; you now have a greater readiness for self-examination and stillness.

Practice: A mindfulness walk is a marvelous way to spend quality time with yourself. Anoint your wrists with jasmine essential oil, which will lift your mood and spirit and bring about a calm and inner peace. Clear your mind and take in the beauty of nature as you walk. You can literally stop and smell the flowers on your wisdom walk.

IX The Hermit

GUIDANCE

Take time away from worldly concerns and focus on your inner life. Get in touch with your truest self. Be in solitude.

X The Wheel of Fortune

Cycles of Transformation

X The Wheel of Fortune

GUIDANCE

Reflect on past cycles to recognize patterns, and move forward with openness to what lies ahead.

This mesmerizing card portrays a spinning wheel woven with vines of ivy and honeysuckle, symbolizing resilience and the sweetness of life's cycles. At its center, a chamomile flower radiates calm amid change. Four elemental creatures—a sparrow (Air), a salamander (Fire), a fish (Water), and a turtle (Earth)—encircle the wheel, representing the balance of nature's forces. In the background, a starry night sky twinkles over a field of swaying wheat, suggesting the ever-turning rhythm of fate and opportunity.

Meaning: The Wheel of Fortune signifies the ebb and flow of life's cycles, where change is the only constant. Rooted in the natural world, it reflects the seasons' turning and the interplay of destiny and choice. While some events are beyond control, your adaptability and trust in the process shape your journey. Embrace the shifts unfolding around you. The Wheel's turn brings opportunities disguised as challenges. Stay grounded, like the turtle, and flexible, like the sparrow's wings. Trust that the Universe is aligning events for your growth.

Practice: Craft a ritual to honor life's cycles. Gather fresh or dried chamomile flowers and a small stone to represent the Earth. Sit under the night sky or near a window while holding the stone and sprinkle the chamomile in a circle. Visualize the wheel of your life turning, bringing lessons and possibilities. Incant an intention for adaptability and trust. Sit in stillness for five minutes, then keep the stone as a reminder to flow with change.

XI Justice
The Blade of Balance

Seated between soaring columns, the figure of Justice wears a simple and noble crown, which is bedecked with one simple flower, the black-eyed Susan or rudbeckia, long held as a symbol of fairness. A sword is held upright in the right hand, representing the sharp blade which slices through questions, indecision, and clouded thinking. In the left hand are scales to balance what is just and right.

Meaning: This is the most weighty and solemn card to land in a reading. Judgment signifies accountability wherein choices you make will reflect upon you and your judgment. Now is the time for important decisions for you, ones that can define your near future. Fairness and truth are the matters at hand. Whether it is a decision you are making or one impacting your life, the sword of Justice cuts through clearly and cleanly to reveal the truth. If there is any situation where you need to make a challenging choice, create balance, or cut something out of your life, you will make the right decision now.

Practice: To help you make choices, take your athame (see page 4) or a knife and place it in a bowl of salt for a full day and a night. The salt will clean and purify the magical tool. Place the blade on your altar or table where you can see it often when key decisions are being made.

GUIDANCE

Justice will prevail. Trust in your inner knowing to make the right choice, as you now have true discernment.

XII The Hanged Man

What Must You Give Up to Grow?

GUIDANCE

Release the need to force outcomes and instead listen to your inner wisdom. Stillness is preparing you for profound growth.

This serene character hangs upside down from an ancient tree. With leafy datura vines entwined around his foot and ankle, he is dressed simply in blue apart from his red stockings, which draw attention to his legs. These form the shape of a cross, a symbol of sacrifice, salvation, and divine protection. A quiet visionary, The Hanged Man embraces stillness, seeing the world from a different perspective. His wisdom lies in patience, revealing hidden truths through surrender. The Hanged Man offers the gift of clarity through release.

Meaning: What must you sacrifice to make personal and spiritual progress? The Hanged Man signifies a time of suspension, where pausing brings deeper understanding. It invites you to let go of control and trust the flow of life's timing. This is a moment to shift your perspective, to find peace in uncertainty, and to embrace the lessons of stillness. The Hanged Man asks you to rest in the beauty of surrender. This card may reflect your own need for pause or the presence of a calm, reflective soul in your life.

Practice: Find what seems to be the oldest tree in your neighborhood, perhaps in a nearby park, or even in your backyard. Sit with your back against the trunk and feel the life thrumming inside the tree, flowing from the roots to the branches and leaves. Trees are the lungs of the planet: Speak aloud your gratitude to ancient trees as you commune together.

XIII Death
Time for Transformation

Soft, golden leaves fall gently from a tree, drifting to the earth. The tree is dying, shedding its leaves—but all around it, new growth is already beginning to appear. New sprouts rise from the soil, vibrant and alive. Above the tree, the cycle of the Moon is portrayed. The Death card is the promise of rebirth.

Meaning: This card arrives with a tender whisper, heralding transformation and renewal. It may reflect an aspect of you ready to release the past or signal the end of a significant chapter. A quiet guide, Death is not to be feared but embraced as a wise companion through change. It holds the secrets of cycles, understanding that every ending births a new beginning, and signifies profound change, where what no longer serves you falls away. It invites you to let go of attachments—be they habits, beliefs, or situations—with grace. Honor what has been while opening your heart to new possibilities. Seek solace from those who support your growth or in quiet reflection.

Practice: Gather a pomegranate, a bowl, and your athame (see page 4) and cut the fruit in two. Take in the beauty of this fruit, which symbolizes the world of the living and the realm beyond. Take three of the seeds and eat them slowly, savoring the deliciousness. Place the fruit on your altar and light a candle to honor life and what comes after.

GUIDANCE

Surrender to transformation, and embrace the beauty of what emerges: Step into the unknown with faith.

The Major Arcana

XIV Temperance
Grace in Balance

Standing at the edge of a tranquil stream, a graceful woman pours water between two clay vessels, one adorned with lavender sprigs and the other with lotus blossoms, symbolizing balance and purity. Her dress shimmers with shades of blue and green, with the sleeves featuring silver sage, reflecting adaptability and calm. A heron stands nearby, poised on one leg, embodying patience and grace. In the background, yarrow and violets stretch toward a soft sunrise.

Meaning: Temperance represents the art of balance, blending opposing forces to create harmony. Like the stream's gentle flow, it encourages patience, moderation, and the integration of your inner and outer worlds. Blend intuition with logic, action with rest, and giving with receiving to make intentional choices. Small, mindful steps will lead to lasting harmony. Like the heron, stand steady amid life's currents.

Practice: Create a ritual to foster balance. Gather lavender and a small vial of water (or use a clear glass). Sit in a quiet space, place the lavender beside you, and hold the water. Visualize yourself pouring energy between two aspects of your life (for example, work and rest). Breathe deeply, imagining these forces merging in harmony. Stand in a state of mindfulness, focusing on balance. Sprinkle a pinch of lavender into the water and keep it as a talisman for calm and clarity.

GUIDANCE

Trust the process of blending contrasts, and seek moderation to align with your higher purpose.

XV The Devil

Learning to Let Go

A horned crown, representing The Devil, can be seen above two people who are bound together by growing vines. The vines are only loosely wrapped around the figures—they could escape if they chose to do so. The short, goat-like horns represent the animal aspect of humanity as well as unbridled natural, physical desires that are a real part of the human psyche.

Meaning: The Devil appears with a quiet intensity: it is a gentle nudge to face what binds you. We forge chains for ourselves through fear, addiction, or limiting beliefs. Explore what keeps you tethered, whether habits, thoughts, or relationships. Wise in the ways of temptation, The Devil knows the allure of such things. Yet this card is not to be feared—it is a teacher, revealing where freedom awaits. Gently confront your fears or dependencies with self-kindness. Seek support from a trusted friend or guide to help you see clearly. This card may reflect an inner struggle or an external force holding you back. It could also herald the arrival of a charismatic yet challenging presence in your life.

Practice: Create a safe space by burning a cinnamon candle and incense, bringing in the energy of abundance and comfort. Sit comfortably, with your spine straight, and take a few deep breaths. Close your eyes. Envision a soft, golden cord wrapped gently around you, representing what binds you. With each exhale, imagine the cord loosening and dissolving into light. Spend time in stillness, affirming your power to release and heal.

GUIDANCE

Look within to see shadows with compassion, and have the courage to release what no longer serves you.

XVI The Tower

Major Change is Nigh

Gentle rain washes over a crumbling stone tower. Despite the devastation taking place, a radiant light is rising powerfully from the base of the tower, illuminating the path which leads the way. Sage, with its cleansing and purifying properties, is growing all around. The Tower represents liberation through upheaval.

Meaning: The Tower appears with a soft yet powerful presence, signaling a moment of profound awakening through unexpected change, where illusions or unstable foundations crumble. It may reflect an inner shift or the sudden collapse of outdated structures in your life. Embrace this disruption as a chance to rebuild with authenticity. The Tower carries the gift of truth, revealing what must change to align with your soul's path. Though its arrival feels intense, this card clears the way for clarity. Release resistance and trust that what falls away makes space for truth and growth. Face change with courage and an open heart, and seek grounding in simple joys or the support of loved ones.

Practice: Take two small bowls and fill one with salt and one with water. Leave them on your altar for a full day and night, so they can remove negative energy from your home. After 24 hours, throw the salt out in the street in front of your home and pour the water onto the salt. Enjoy the newly clarified energy of your home.

GUIDANCE

Find strength in surrendering to life's transformative currents. This is a sacred opportunity to realign with your higher purpose.

XVII The Star
Lighting Your Way Forward

The Star shines softly in your reading, a beacon of hope and serenity. She is both a celestial figure, carrying the wisdom of the cosmos, as well as a very human woman, kneeling at a body of water under a star-strewn sky. Behind her is an idyllic meadow, verdant with herbs and grasses. The woman, skyclad under the glow of the many stars, pours the water of wisdom into the pool.

Meaning: This card signifies a period of restoration, where wounds mend and clarity emerges. After challenges, you're invited to bask in the gentle glow of possibility. Seek out sources of inspiration—perhaps a mentor or the beauty of nature—to guide your heart. Trust the Universe's flow, let go of fear, and embrace the quiet beauty of your journey. The Star asks you to nurture your dreams with patience and faith, whispering that you are never alone. She may reflect your own emerging inner light or signal the arrival of a kind, inspiring figure who offers solace.

Practice: Find a quiet moment one evening to connect with the stars. Gather a blossom from a night-blooming flower, such as fragrant lily or jasmine, as they inspire wonder. Step outside or sit by a window, gazing at the night sky. Take slow, deep breaths, feeling the air fill your lungs with calm. Close your eyes and picture a radiant silver star glowing within your chest. Visualize its light spreading, soothing every part of you. Spend 11 minutes (11 is a master number—see the Practice on page 16) in this gentle meditation daily to renew your spirit.

XVII The Star

GUIDANCE

Believe in your resilience and let hope lead you toward peace.

The Major Arcana

XVIII The Moon

Revealing What Was Hidden

On a plain surrounded by water, a white dog and a large black feline look up at a luminous full moon. Salmon also emerge from the water to gaze at the orb in the night sky. The plain is surrounded by night-blooming 'Casa Blanca' lilies, whose large, white flowers echo the glow of the Moon above.

Meaning: Luna, or The Moon, is about change, and focuses in particular on what is unknown and cannot yet be seen, just as the dark side of the Moon is not visible to us. Mysterious and filled with portent, The Moon embodies matters of intuition and imagination, as well as illusion and fantasy. You may be entering a period of change in your life with a sense of great trepidation. Don't let your imagination get carried away or allow fears and blocks to get in your way. Follow your real intuition, your true inner guidance, and use that as a rudder in your life.

Practice: Designate a blank journal to be your dream journal. Lay a sprig of rosemary in a small dish on your nightstand. Rosemary will help you remember your dreams and is redolent with healing energy. When you awaken in the morning, write down your dreams, the wisdom that came to you in the night as you slept under the light of the Moon.

GUIDANCE

Tap into your inner awareness—
your path ahead will be clear and
right for you.

XIX The Sun
Radiance and Vitality

Bathed in the glow of a brilliant sun, a striking figure stands with arms outstretched with marigold and chamomile blossoms before them, symbols of optimism and healing. A playful fox dances nearby, its fur gleaming with warmth, embodying vitality and cunning joy. Towering sunflowers sway in the background, their faces turned toward the light, while a clear blue sky sparkles above, radiating boundless energy and clarity.

Meaning: The Sun shines with unbridled joy and success. It represents a time of clarity, vitality, and alignment with your true self. This card is about the life-giving force of nature, urging you to embrace positivity, confidence, and authentic expression. Bask in the light of your own potential. Like the fox, move with playful confidence and trust that clarity will guide your path. Share your warmth with others and let optimism fuel your next steps.

Practice: Harness radiant energy using a marigold flower (or a small, yellow item) and a piece of citrine or a clear stone. Sit in sunlight or near a bright light, holding the marigold and crystal/stone. Visualize golden light filling your body, igniting joy and confidence. Breathe deeply, affirming, "I shine with my true light." For a few minutes, focus on a moment of pure happiness. Carry the stone as a talisman to radiate positivity.

GUIDANCE
Celebrate your achievements and let your inner spark shine.

XX Judgment
Awakening and Renewal

GUIDANCE

Move forward with courage, knowing you are ready to embody your higher purpose.

Rising from a bed of lush ferns, an angelic being stretches her arms toward the sky. Her robe is adorned with sprigs of angelica and hyssop, which symbolize purification and spiritual awakening. A majestic owl, its wings spread wide, perches nearby, clutching a branch of mugwort, an herb of wisdom and intuition. Around the luminous figure, white lilies bloom under a radiant dawn, evoking rebirth and clarity of purpose.

Meaning: Judgment heralds a profound awakening, calling you to rise above past limitations and embrace your higher purpose. At this moment of reckoning, reflection leads to transformation. Listen carefully to the call within you. Release old patterns, forgive yourself, and embrace your authentic path. Like the owl, trust your intuition to guide you toward clarity. Reflect on your journey and acknowledge your growth.

Practice: In order to accept the spiritual awakening you are about to experience, you need to cleanse your space and your personal energy. Hyssop is a wonderful herb to do just that. Brew a pot of hyssop tea, using a palmful of the dried herb. Pour the tea into a cup, then take a clean white cloth and dip it into the warm water. Use the cloth to wipe down all the doorknobs, windowsills, tables, and anywhere else in your home you think needs negative energy removed. Sweep the front and back entrances to your home and pour the rest of the pot of hyssop tea outside both doors.

XXI The World

Honor the End of a Cycle

The World depicts a woman experiencing liberation after a long effort and success from a cycle of energetic work. The celebratory aspect of the card is to honor that positive and fruitful cycle. Through the lens of green witchery, this is a time of harvesting all the seeds for success you planted. Your garden bursts with beauty and life-giving vegetables, herbs, fruits, nuts, and berries, which all can enjoy.

Meaning: You have completed a full cycle of your life and should enjoy the fruits of your labor. Drawing this card is an indication that you are wrapping up a phase of your life. Now is the time to enjoy the benefits of your sustained effort and energy. You are in a liminal period where you can rest, acknowledge your bounty, be recognized by the world, and reap the benefits of what you have accomplished in the cycle of your life that has just ended. You need to honor and process that cycle to help you prepare for the new phase to come.

Practice: Incorporating the reaping and harvesting energy of this card is an important way to stay connected to the Earth. Plant a tree that bears fruit or nuts in your garden or deck space, whether it is a lemon tree in a big handsome pot on your front porch, herbs on a sunny windowsill, an apple tree out back, or a grapevine growing on the fence. Tend your new planting lovingly and you will reap what you have sown.

XXI The World

GUIDANCE

Be grateful for the significant time in your life which has just ended, along with all the lessons learned and new experiences it brought you.

The Minor Arcana

The cards of the Minor Arcana are divided into four suits. Within each suit there are 14 cards—the "pip" cards from Ace to Ten and the court cards of Page, Knight, Queen, and King.

The suits feature plants that reflect their meanings:

- **The suit of Crystals (Pentacles/Coins)**, tied to wealth and resources, showcases daisies and ivy with the pips as crystal balls. It is connected to the element of Earth.
- **The suit of Athames (Swords)**, depicted by the green witch's magical knife and sunflowers, represents mental clarity. It is connected to the element of Air.
- **The suit of Wands** channels creative energy through budding branches against vibrant apple trees. It is connected to the element of Fire.
- **The suit of Goblets (Cups)** evokes emotions with silverware decorated with poppies and a lavender background. It is connected to the element of Water.

On the following pages you will find a description of each card's meaning, as well as a practice which can be used to channel the particular energy of that card.

Ace of Crystals

Heralding new beginnings in wealth, health, or stability, this card shows clear potential for prosperity. It represents a seed of opportunity in the material realm, inviting you to nurture financial or physical growth. Plant intentions with care and trust in abundance. In green witchery, it aligns with Earth's generative energy, amplified by the crystal ball's clarity.

Practice: Plant a profusion of daisies to add the abundance of the Ace of Crystals to your life. Tend the plants, visualizing prosperity growing steadily with each leaf.

Two of Crystals

This card represents balance, adaptability, and juggling valuable resources or responsibilities, and it mirrors nature's rhythmic cycles. It indicates crystalline clarity in managing your time, finances, or energy, while focusing on what needs tending. However, be flexible to maintain harmony amid various demands.

Practice: Brew a balancing tea with dried lavender and lemon balm, herbs for calm and focus. Steep them, visualizing equilibrium in your tasks. Store the blend in a jar with an amethyst crystal to enhance clarity. Sip daily to ground your energy and support poised, clear decision-making.

Three of Crystals

The themes of this card are teamwork, skill development, and collaborative success, just as nature's systems are interconnected, too. There is a shared vision, mastered through group effort—it is about fostering unity to build something enduring together.

Practice: Create an altar using small stones painted with unity symbols (like interlocking circles). Arrange the stones in a circle with a central patch of vervain, an herb of cooperation. Place a rose quartz crystal in the center to amplify harmony. Tend to the altar regularly to strengthen collective goals and bonds.

Four of Crystals

This card reflects security, control, and clinging to resources, sometimes fearfully. It reveals the need for inner motivation, warning against stagnation and urging trust that abundance will come. Reflect on what you are holding tightly. In green witchery, the card connects to Earth's stability.

Practice: Perform a release ritual using willow leaves, symbols of flexibility. Using a gel pen or nontoxic marker pen, write down your fears of loss on the leaves, then burn them safely in a fireproof bowl, visualizing freedom. Scatter the ashes in soil with tiger's eye crystal chips for courage, planting trust in Earth's abundant provision.

Five of Crystals

Financial or spiritual hardship, isolation, or lack are indicated here. However, the card also suggests hidden hope, urging you to find resilience and seek support. This card reflects vulnerability but also renewal—just like nature's healing cycles.

Practice: Reconnect to the Earth's nurturing energy and ease feelings of scarcity and isolation by crafting a talisman to wear. Wrap a sunstone crystal, which radiates vitality, in a cloth with dried nettle for strength, then charge it in sunlight. Carry the crystal with you to attract hope and resilience during challenges.

Six of Crystals

This card embodies generosity, balanced exchange, and sharing resources. It illuminates fairness in giving and receiving, fostering harmony, and reflects abundance through kindness. Just as a sprig of ivy can grow and cover an entire wall, so can the spirit of generosity spread throughout your life.

Practice: Chamomile is associated with kindness. Plant a chamomile cutting and set intentions to share positivity as you nurture it. Once grown, harvest and dry the flowers, creating sachets with a peridot crystal to give to others. This ritual cultivates a cycle of generosity rooted in the Earth's abundant spirit.

Seven of Crystals

The themes of this card are patience, long-term investment, and evaluating progress. This is about steady outcomes and encourages trust in slow growth—just like nature's gradual cycles. Reflect on your efforts.

Practice: Sow calendula seeds, symbolizing endurance, in a small plot. Tend them mindfully, reflecting on your goals as they grow. Place a green aventurine crystal nearby to amplify growth. Journal your progress beside the plants, grounding your patience in nature's rhythm for long-term success.

Eight of Crystals

This card signifies diligence, skill refinement, and dedication to craft with a clear focus and precision. Celebrate effort and mastery: This card promises rewards for hard work.

Practice: Choose a fresh branch that has fallen to the ground as your new wand, symbolizing growth. Sand and polish the wand, meditating on your skills. Place it in your workspace with a fluorite crystal for focus. This ritual enhances concentration, grounding your craftsmanship in nature's steady guidance and fostering skill development.

Nine of Crystals

Enjoy the fruits of your labor: This card denotes both self-sufficiency and luxury. Key themes are personal abundance, confidence, gratitude, and achievement. In green witchery, this card connects to nature's harvest.

Practice: Get seed packets of nine different types and colors of daisies. Plant them in the spring to draw toward you the profusion of abundance in the Nine of Crystals. Observe the daisies as they grow and reflect on your blessings, deepening your connection to the Earth's generous gifts.

Ten of Crystals

Legacy, family wealth, and long-term stability are the themes of this card. Reflecting community and enduring success, it celebrates shared prosperity and generational efforts.

Practice: Plant a hazel tree sapling to honor generational growth. Bless it with water infused with bay leaves for prosperity, setting intentions for community strength. Place a smoky quartz crystal at the base of the sapling to ground your vision. Tend the tree as a living legacy, fostering collective abundance.

Page of Crystals

A figure of youth and hope, the Page of Crystals indicates a fresh beginning in your life. As this card steps into your reading, it may signal that you will take up a new study or explore new aspects of work; it is definitely a time of newfound abundance in your life, with more money and security. As the Page gazes into the crystal ball, so should you consider what potential lies ahead for you and be open to the positive and the new.

Practice: Enhance the abundance coming your way by burning cinnamon incense on your altar and in your bedroom, so your home is infused with the energy of prosperity.

Knight of Crystals

Embodying steadfast progress and relentless dedication, this Knight shows you how to stand strong. You are called to chase goals with patience and practicality, forging abundance through steady effort. Trust your vision, stay rooted, and let resilience lead the way. Gazing into a garnet crystal ball, brimming with energy and vitality, the Knight sees dreams take shape. Replace doubts such as "I can't do this" with "I build success step by step."

Practice: Take a long sprig of ivy and lay it out lengthwise over your desk or altar. Its vibrant energy sparks gratitude, attracting prosperity. Your path is blooming brilliantly.

Queen of Crystals

This queenly figure arrives in your reading as a grounded, earthy goddess. The soul of abundance, she is a reminder of the good life and how you can achieve that through a practical and centered approach to life, nurturing yourself, and being able to receive as well as give. Now, you should pay attention to domestic affairs and the comforts of home and garden, as well as familial and romantic relationships. Her vision-boosting amethyst crystal ball holds a vision of your contented life of creature comforts and cozy security.

Practice: Add prosperity elements to your home altar nightstand by adding a dish with a small amethyst crystal.

King of Crystals

Money is a main consideration when this powerful figure appears in your reading and his mission is to steer you toward becoming more responsible in your life, in a grounded, practical, and more serious way. Take your finances by the horn and set the foundation for a life of wealth, ease, and comfort. In his peridot crystal ball, the King of Crystals sees for you a future of abundant living. You have arrived at a place in your life where you need to step up and accept responsibility for your own prospects; what are your ambitions?

Practice: Take a blank book and start journaling a wish list for your future. Keep it by your bedside.

Ace of Athames

This Ace ignites raw potential and new beginnings. Picture a gleaming athame, its blade piercing the air in a sunlit sunflower field, symbolizing untapped intellect and courage. Expect a surge of mental clarity, enabling you to embrace fresh ideas and assert your willpower with confidence. This marks the start of a journey fueled by determination. Let the sunflowers' radiant energy guide your path.

Practice: Write a bold thought on paper, bury it beneath a sunflower, and visualize its roots growing strong, nurturing your mind with clear, creative energy.

Two of Athames

This card reflects duality and tough choices. Pulling this card points to a need for balance between intellect and emotion. This card invites you to weigh options with care, trusting your inner wisdom to resolve tension. The sunflowers stand for resilience in uncertainty. Swap indecision for clarity.

Practice: Create a decision chart with pros and cons, place it in sunlight, and meditate on it to charge your mind with clarity and focused energy.

Three of Athames

Heartache and division are signified here. Seeing this card warns of misunderstandings or a fractured mind needing healing. Look to collaboration to mend rifts, using shared intellect to find harmony. The sunflowers offer hope amid strife. Embrace unity.

Practice: Stand barefoot on the earth, holding a sunflower, and visualize your ideas expanding like petals. Breathe deeply, grounding your thoughts in nature's enduring strength.

Four of Athames

There is a time of peace and rest after turmoil. This card indicates recovery from mental exhaustion, urging a pause to regain focus. Let tranquility restore your mind's sharpness, trusting in the stability you've built. The sunflowers symbolize calm renewal.

Practice: Sit in silence with a marigold flower, inhaling its scent. Visualize your mind clearing, renewing your sharpness and preparing you for the challenges that lie ahead.

The Minor Arcana

Five of Athames

Conflict, tension, and competition: This card highlights rivalry or inner struggle, urging you to channel disputes into growth. Embrace any challenges as catalysts for clarity, letting the sunflowers' resilience guide you. Swap discord for insight.

Practice: Burn sage in a fireproof dish, cleansing your space of negativity. Visualize the smoke carrying away confusion, leaving a sharpened focus for constructive and innovative solutions.

Six of Athames

Celebrate victory and recognition. You are overcoming adversity through intellect and effort. This card urges you to share your wisdom confidently, inspiring others with your success. The sunflowers symbolize the blossoming of achievement.

Practice: Wear a citrine necklace, letting its uplifting energy amplify your clarity. Visualize your successes blooming like radiant sunflowers, guiding your next steps with purpose and illuminating your path forward.

Seven of Athames

Customarily, this card warns of opposition and urges you to protect your beliefs with resilience. Find courage under pressure and swap doubt for determination. The sunflowers offer enduring strength.

Practice: Hold an obsidian stone, feeling its grounding weight. Visualize a shield around your thoughts, bolstering your resolve with unyielding focus to defend your intellectual territory.

Eight of Athames

This card's themes are swift action and transition. Traditionally, it marks rapid change or movement, urging you to seize opportunities with precision. Picture the blades of the athames cutting through stagnation with decisive thought, and let the sunflowers' dynamic growth inspire bold progress.

Practice: Light some sandalwood incense, letting its rising smoke mirror your swift thoughts. Meditate on its positive, calming scent while visualizing your ideas soaring freely toward success with unstoppable momentum.

The Minor Arcana

Nine of Athames

You are nearing your goals through resilience. This card signifies perseverance through hardship, urging you to trust your intuition despite fatigue. The sunflowers embody tenacity. Swap exhaustion for resolve.

Practice: Brew some chamomile tea, sipping slowly to refresh your mind. Chamomile brings peace. Visualize its warmth renewing your energy and fueling your resolve to think clearly and pursue your path with vigor.

Ten of Athames

The Ten symbolizes the end of a circle. Here, the card warns of mental overload. You are urged to release excess responsibilities and reclaim clarity. The sunflowers remind you to lighten your load. Swap burden for freedom.

Practice: Write down overwhelming thoughts on pieces of paper, then burn them safely in a fireproof bowl. Visualize the smoke freeing your mind for a lighter, more vibrant intellectual journey.

Page of Athames

This card heralds curiosity and new learning. In a sunlit field, a youthful figure holds an athame, its blade gleaming among vibrant sunflowers, symbolizing the start of a mental quest. This Page represents a message or opportunity to expand your knowledge, urging you to approach challenges with an open, eager mind. The sunflowers embody optimism and growth, encouraging you to embrace this fresh perspective. Swap hesitation for enthusiasm as you step into intellectual exploration.

Practice: Yellow represents positivity and the color of the Sun, which is tracked devotedly by sunflowers. Light a yellow candle surrounded by sage leaves, meditate for five minutes, and visualize your mind blooming with new ideas and insights.

Page of Athames

Knight of Athames

When you see this man galloping into your reading, it means that change is afoot and you are entering a very busy time in your life. You should take a moment to pause and reflect on current circumstances and see if you are being overly aggressive in any way, perhaps pushing or trying too hard. Drawing this card can also mean that, whatever needs doing, you have the high energy and verve to get it done. The orange and yellow sunflowers represent the strength and optimism of this court card.

Practice: This Knight symbolizes strength, determination, and confidence. Connect with these attributes by burning a candle which has been dressed (anointed) with bergamot essential oil—add a couple of drops of oil to the side of the candle using a dropper or cotton ball.

Knight of Athames

Queen of Athames

Clarity and clear thinking is the order of the day when this Queen lands in your reading; she is counseling you to take care and not be overly persuaded by emotions: Remain calm and tap into your inner knowing. If you use your personal wisdom, it will guide you safely and serenely at a time when outside voices, who might not be completely honest, are trying to influence you. Listen and hold fast to your inner voice, and you will be safe and composed, just like this Queen on her beautiful throne.

Practice: Choose a chair in your home or garden space as your throne and adorn it with beautiful floral scarves. When you need to get in touch with your inner wisdom and strength, sit on your throne.

King of Athames

This noble figure is here to encourage you to use your mind to overcome challenges in the present or near future; your intellect, along with your good common sense, can see you through what is to come. The King of Athames also urges you to be fair when thinking something through and making a decision. If you are called upon to speak, be honest. You may need to take up your athame and cut something out of your life, or part ways with a person or situation in your life.

Practice: Sunflowers, which are devoted to the Sun, have a vibration of effusive cheerfulness and joy. Connect with their energy by getting up at sunrise and praying for insight and inner guidance.

Ace of Wands

A spark of divine inspiration blazes with this Ace. Seize creative opportunities and trust yourself, ready for new beginnings. Let passion guide your path as you plant seeds for bold ventures. Embrace the courage to start anew, fueled by enthusiasm.

Practice: Apples are bringers of luck, love, and longevity. Write your boldest dream on paper, bury it beneath an apple tree, and visualize its roots growing strong, nurturing your vision with vibrant, creative energy.

Ace of Wands

Two of Wands

This card beckons you to plan with bold vision. Balance ambition with foresight, mapping your path with courage. Swap hesitation for confident steps toward your dreams, trusting your inner compass. The budding wands symbolize potential waiting to bloom through decisive action. Embrace your power to shape the future.

Practice: Create a vision board with images of your goals, place it under moonlight, and meditate on it to charge your intentions with clarity and inspired energy.

Two of Wands

The Minor Arcana

Three of Wands

Possibility lies ahead of you: The Three of Wands radiates expansive vision and progress. This card urges you to trust your efforts, as seeds planted now bloom into opportunities. Embrace collaboration and bold exploration, letting your inner fire illuminate new paths. The budding wands signify growth and forward momentum.

Practice: Stand barefoot on the earth, holding an apple, and visualize your goals expanding like branches. Breathe deeply, grounding your ambitions in nature's strength to fuel your journey.

Four of Wands

This card celebrates harmony and joyful milestones. You are invited to honor achievements, embrace community, and revel in stability. Let gratitude fuel your creative spark, trusting your efforts have built a strong foundation. The budding wands symbolize growth rooted in joy and connection. Share your light, igniting shared dreams.

Practice: Gather friends for a small ritual of sharing wishes. Come together in a circle and pass an apple around; when each person holds the apple, they state their wish. Infuse the moment with gratitude, letting collective energy amplify your celebratory spirit.

Five of Wands

Fiery passion, dynamic tension, and creative conflict are the themes of this card. Channel rivalry into growth, embracing challenges as catalysts for innovation. Swap frustration for collaboration, in pursuit of harmony. The budding wands symbolize potential amid struggle.

Practice: Centering yourself can prepare you for anything life throws at you, including what is brought by the Five of Wands. Go outside and find your favorite nearby tree. Take off your shoes and stand by the tree while gazing up to the top of it. Feel the stability of the roots and take that in as you recenter yourself.

Six of Wands

This card celebrates your triumphs and achievements, urging you to embrace confidence and inspire others. Here, success is rooted in passion and perseverance. Let your true self shine, trusting your journey's progress. Share your light, igniting collective joy.

Practice: Wear a carnelian stone necklace, letting its warm energy amplify your confidence. Stand tall, visualize your successes blooming like apple blossoms, and carry this vibrant energy into your next bold steps.

Seven of Wands

Fierce determination is ignited by this card. Defend your dreams with courage, trusting your inner strength to rise above obstacles. Swap doubt for resilience, letting passion fuel your stand. The budding wands symbolize unwavering potential amid adversity.

Practice: Hematite is a grounding crystal. Hold the stone and visualize a protective shield around your goals, channeling its strength to bolster your resolve and ignite bold, unyielding steps forward.

Eight of Wands

This card signals swift momentum and rapid progress, urging you to seize opportunities and trust the flow of inspiration. Let go of hesitation, embracing the rush of creative action. The budding wands symbolize dynamic growth and unstoppable drive. Move boldly, fueled by passion.

Practice: In order to be nimble and prepared for change and swift action, foster preparedness with walking meditations. Take a stroll through a nearby park to bond with nature and gather Mother Nature's endurance and support.

Nine of Wands

Persevere, with resilience and endurance. You are urged to trust yourself, pushing through challenges with unwavering courage. Swap exhaustion for determination, knowing your goals are near. Remember that strength is forged through trials.

Practice: You can draw upon your considerable inner strength by using affirmations. Cut nine strips of paper and write down a great thing about yourself on each one. Put the pieces of paper in a bowl on your nightstand. Pull out one every morning and say it aloud. Affirm yourself!

Ten of Wands

Be aware of your heavy burdens. This card urges you to reassess your load, releasing what no longer serves your passion. Potential is now strained by too many responsibilities. Swap overwhelm for clarity, and prioritize your creative spark to lighten your path.

Practice: Fend off pressure and external negativity with a protective rite: Burn cinnamon incense for a sense of relaxation, good luck, and an upbeat energy shift.

Page of Wands

This court card sparkles with creative fire and boundless enthusiasm. Against a backdrop of lush hills, the Page holds a wand—a budding apple tree branch—bursting with promise. You are invited to ignite your passions, explore bold ideas, and embrace new adventures with a joyful heart. Swap fears such as "I'm not ready" for "I am bursting with potential."

Practice: Hold an apple, feeling its weight and promise. Take a bite, savoring its sweetness, and let it inspire bold, creative steps toward your goals.

Knight of Wands

Ignite your inner fire with the fearless passion of the Knight of Wands. Despite stormy skies, the Knight charges forward, wielding a wand which is brimming with life. This card beckons you to seize inspiration, act boldly, and pursue your dreams with relentless zeal. Trust your vibrant energy, stay focused, and let courage light your way.

Practice: Light a candle, its flame echoing your inner spark. Sit with its glow, letting its warmth fuel confident steps toward your goals.

Queen of Wands

This luminous Queen glows with creative zeal and magnetic charisma. The essence of inspiration, she urges you to harness your inner drive, lead with unwavering confidence, and chase your dreams fearlessly. Now is the time to spark ambitious goals, trust your instincts, and radiate bold, dynamic energy in all pursuits. Her budding apple staff scepter, a symbol of vitality and courage, guides you toward spirited self-expression and leadership. Embrace her fiery spirit to illuminate your path.

Practice: Place an orange or orange blossom and a citrine crystal on your workspace altar to channel creativity, confidence, and radiant energy into your projects.

King of Wands

This courageous King enters your reading with fearless passion and dynamic energy. The nobleman strikes a magisterial figure, with oak tree branches surrounding his throne. This card urges you to embrace bold action, chase inspiration, and fearlessly pursue your dreams. Swap doubts such as "I'm too reckless" for "I ignite my path with courage."

Practice: Druids held the oak tree sacred and, indeed, oak trees hold a power all their own of fortitude, wisdom, protection, and a long life of peace and prosperity. Collect acorns for your altar as a reminder that each one contains a mighty oak inside.

The Minor Arcana

Ace of Goblets

This card overflows with emotional renewal and heralds new heartfelt beginnings. You are urged to embrace intuition and open your heart to the power of compassion. Let love and creativity flow freely, nurturing soulful connections.

Practice: Carve a heart shape in a lavender-scented candle. Light the candle and place it in a fireproof dish in the room where you spend the most time. Let the lavender inbue your space with tranquility.

Two of Goblets

Heartfelt connection and mutual love are the themes of this card. Can you deepen your relationships, trust emotional harmony, and embrace vulnerability? Swap fear for openness, letting intuition guide your partnerships. Nurture love with courage and compassion, fostering soulful bonds.

Practice: Fill a small, fabric pouch with dried lavender, carry it close, and visualize it radiating love. Hold it during quiet moments to strengthen emotional ties and invite harmony into your relationships.

Three of Goblets

The Three of Goblets celebrates emotional joy and community. This card urges you to revel in shared happiness, nurture friendships, and trust your heart's warmth. Embrace connection through collective love and let gratitude flow.

Practice: Create a gratitude journal, writing down three things you cherish about loved ones and placing a lavender sprig inside. Reflect on these entries to amplify emotional joy and strengthen soulful bonds.

Three of Goblets

Four of Goblets

With whispers of emotional reflection, this card urges you to pause, reassess your heart's needs, and seek deeper fulfillment. Swap apathy for introspection, trusting intuition to guide your path. You can find emotional clarity amid stillness: Embrace quiet moments to rediscover your soul's desires.

Practice: Add four drops of lavender essential oil to a warm bath. While you soak in the infused water, visualize any emotional fog lifting. Let the soothing heat and serene scent cleanse your spirit, renewing your heart's focus and intuitive connection to your deepest aspirations.

Four of Goblets

The Minor Arcana

Five of Goblets

The Five of Goblets mourns emotional loss. This card urges you to grieve, yet seek healing through remaining love. Swap despair for gentle acceptance, trusting your heart's resilience. The lavender signifies clarity amid sorrow.

Practice: The color white represents new beginnings, healing, and self-understanding. Light a white candle, place lavender petals around it, and meditate on its glow. Visualize healing light mending your heart, fostering a period of emotional recovery and renewed hope for soulful connections ahead.

Six of Goblets

This card evokes nostalgic warmth and emotional renewal. Reconnect with past joys, nurture innocence, and heal old wounds with love. Trust your heart's memories to guide you toward emotional harmony. Embrace heartfelt bonds and your inner child's light.

Practice: Lavender is a powerful herb for dreamwork. Place dried lavender in an envelope with a piece of paper, then put it under your pillow before bedtime. While you sleep, the herb will bring deep, peaceful slumber with illuminating dreams. Upon waking, write down what you can remember on the piece of paper and reflect upon the meaning of your nighttime visions.

Seven of Goblets

You are facing emotional choices. This card urges you to discern true desires from illusions, trusting intuition to guide your heart. Swap confusion for clarity, focusing on soulful aspirations.

Practice: Hold an amethyst crystal, close your eyes, and breathe deeply. Visualize each goblet revealing a heartfelt goal, letting the crystal's energy clear confusion and amplify your intuition to choose paths aligned with your soul's deepest desires.

Seven of Goblets

Eight of Goblets

This card signals emotional departure. You are urged to release what no longer serves your heart, trusting your intuition to guide you to new paths and seek deeper fulfillment. Swap stagnation for courage, embracing soulful transformation. There is clarity in letting go. Move toward renewal with faith.

Practice: Write a letter to release past emotions, sprinkle it with lavender oil, and bury it under a tree. Visualize your heart lightening, so you can embrace new emotional horizons with clarity and courage.

Eight of Goblets

Nine of Goblets

This card celebrates emotional fulfillment and your heart's desires realized. Savor joy and gratitude for the emotional abundance you have to inspire others. Bask in your heart's warmth.

Practice: Create a rosewater spray (rose nurtures the heart), mist your space, and inhale its scent. Visualize joy blooming like roses, amplifying your emotional contentment and inviting deeper gratitude into your heart's radiant fulfillment.

Ten of Goblets

Soulful unity and emotional harmony abound. Cherish love, family, and community. Swap doubt for gratitude, trusting your heart's fullness. Embrace love's radiant bonds.

Practice: Plant poppy seeds in a pot, naming each for a loved one. Tend to the seeds daily, visualizing your connections growing stronger, fostering emotional harmony and deep gratitude for your soulful, interconnected community.

Page of Goblets

This poetic and youthful figure stands by the ocean, clutching a goblet overflowing with colorful nasturtiums. Clad in a vibrant aquamarine waistcoat adorned with the same vibrant flowers, he embodies emotional curiosity and intuitive dreams. This Page invites you to explore your heart's whispers with confidence, embrace sensitivity, and dive into creative inspiration. Now is the time to nurture your imagination and trust your inner voice.

Practice: Place a nasturtium flower and a small aquamarine crystal on your nightstand or bedside altar to foster intuitive dreams and emotional clarity.

Knight of Goblets

This radiant blonde Knight rides a white horse through a vibrant poppy field, her goblet brimming with water and fragrant lavender. Her cloak, embroidered with poppies, flows as she journeys toward a shimmering lake, embodying emotional quests and soulful devotion. She inspires you to chase dreams with compassion and courage and to trust your intuition. Now, embrace romantic ideals and heartfelt connections. Her lavender-filled goblet symbolizes emotional depth and clarity.

Practice: Sit beneath a tree, holding a vial of water with lavender flowers in it, and meditate on your heart's desires to deepen intuitive connections and emotional harmony.

The Minor Arcana **63**

Queen of Goblets

Embodying deep intuition and emotional wisdom, this serene Queen sits by a vast lake, cradling a large goblet in both hands. Her grand throne is decorated with white roses, while her ocean-blue robes and magnificent crown, adorned with a white lily, mirror the throne's elegance. She urges you to embrace compassion, nurture your heart, and trust your inner vision. Now is the time to foster soulful connections and emotional healing.

Practice: Brew some rose petal tea, a heart-healing herb, and sip it mindfully by a window, reflecting on love and emotional renewal under a tree's gentle shade.

King of Goblets

This majestic King sits by the water, overseeing his navy, clad in purple and gold robes adorned with lavender patterns. Holding a scepter in one hand and a goblet blooming with lavender in the other, he embodies emotional mastery and compassionate leadership. He urges you to balance your heart and mind, guiding others with wisdom and empathy. Now, nurture deep connections and emotional stability. His lavender-filled goblet radiates calm and clarity.

Practice: Light lavender incense by a window, envisioning emotional harmony, and breathe deeply to inspire compassionate decisions.